ASTROLOGY

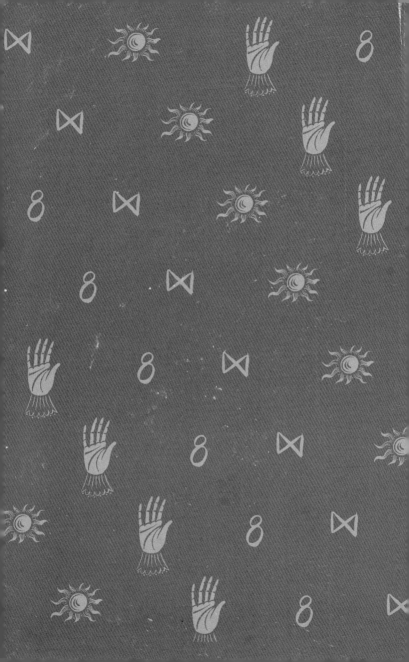

© Element Books Limited 2000

First published in Great Britain in 2000 by
ELEMENT BOOKS LIMITED
Shaftesbury, Dorset SP7 8BP

Published in the USA in 2000 by
ELEMENT BOOKS INC.
160 North Washington Street, Boston MA 02114

Published in Australia in 2000 by
ELEMENT BOOKS
and distributed by Penguin Australia Ltd.
487 Maroondah Highway, Ringwood, Victoria 3134

Designed and created for Element Books with
The Bridgewater Book Company

ELEMENT BOOKS LIMITED
Editorial Director *Sue Hook*
Senior Commissioning Editor *Caro Ness*
Project Manager *Shirley Patton*
Group Production Director *Clare Armstrong*
Production Manager *Stephanie Raggett*
Production Controller *Hannah Turner*

THE BRIDGEWATER BOOK COMPANY
Art Director *Terry Jeavons*
Designer *Alison Honey*
Editorial Director *Fiona Biggs*
Managing Editor *Anne Townley*
Project Editor *Caroline Earle*
Picture Research *Lynda Marshall*
Illustrations *Alice Englander*
Endpapers *Sarah Young*

Printed and bound in Portugal

British Library Cataloguing in Publication
data available

Library of Congress Cataloging in Publication data available

ISBN: 1-86204-483-X

Picture credits:

Bridgeman Art Library: 5t (O'Shea Gallery, London), 7r, (Louvre, Paris), 39 (Glasgow Art
Galleries & Museum), 42 (Pinacoteca di Brera, Milan), 46 (City of Bristol Museum & Art
Gallery, Avon). *Image Bank*: 8, 15, 17b, 19, 21, 23, 25b, 27, 29b, 31, 33b, 35, 37b.

ASTROLOGY

LORI REID

ELEMENT

Shaftesbury, Dorset • Boston, Massachusetts • Melbourne, Victoria

CONTENTS

WHAT IS ASTROLOGY?

Astrologers believe that the patterns in the heavens directly mirror the patterns on Earth. As above, so below. Astrology, which means "the study of the stars," looks at the relationship between planetary movements and events happening on Earth.

OUR DAILY LIVES

 The stars in the night sky have been observed for many thousands of years. Each planet has been ascribed a set of characteristics that are activated, modified, or enhanced according to the relationships it makes with other planets on its orbit around the Sun. Some of the relationships are stressful, but others are harmonious, and it is patterns like these, changing constantly from day to day, that reflect the challenging situations that take place in our lives.

Because the celestial patterns can be calculated with precision for days, weeks, and even years in advance, astrologers are able to make predictions about future events.

A SHORT HISTORY

 Some believe that astrology was practiced in legendary Atlantis thousands of years before the birth of Christ. Certainly, the stars have long been studied by mystics and seers, and cyclical events such as the phases of the Moon and motions of the planets were recognized and recorded as far back as the dawn of civilization.

But we do know that detailed records of planetary movements, eclipses, and returning comets were made by the Babylonians. Later, records show that the people of Mesopotamia refined this knowledge, and some of the first tangible evidence of the practice of astrology

THE RELATIONSHIPS THE PLANETS MAKE WITH EACH OTHER
ARE CENTRAL TO THE STUDY OF ASTROLOGY.

comes from Chaldea some 3,000 years B.C.E. Here, the mechanism of the solar system was recognized, the visible planets identified, and the signs of the Zodiac as we know them today were named and characterized. In fact, for thousands of years, astrologers were known as Chaldeans.

THE HOROSCOPE

Taken from a Greek word meaning "the observation of time," a horoscope is a map of the heavens charting the positions of the planets at any specific moment. Usually drawn up for the birth of a baby, or to mark the beginning of an event, the horoscope "freeze-frames" the celestial patterns that are believed to represent a particular nativity. Interpreting these patterns will describe the character of that child or event, and show the influences most likely to affect the course of its life.

A horoscope, or birth chart, may be drawn up to give insight into the outcome of a marriage, a new business venture, a long journey, financial investment, or moving house.

IN ASTROLOGY THE
TIME OF BIRTH
HOLDS THE
KEY.

A REPRESENTATION OF THE
ZODIACAL CIRCLE AROUND
THE EARTH.

A REPRESENTATION OF THE
ZODIACAL CIRCLE AROUND
THE EARTH.

THE ZODIAC

 The Zodiac is an imaginary band in the sky that encircles the Earth along which the astrological planets "appear" to move. The word (from Greek) means a "ring of animals" and refers to the 12 signs that begin with Aries the Ram and end with Pisces the Fish. Each sign spans a 30-degree segment of this band and collectively the twelve form a 360-degree band, making up the complete zodiacal circle.

Scientifically, of course, it is the planets that are orbiting around the Sun in our solar system, but from Earth it looks as if it is the Sun and the planets that are moving around us. As they encircle the Earth, the planets seem to travel along that imaginary zodiacal band, proceeding at their different speeds through the twelve signs in turn.

SUN SIGNS

 If you are a Leo or Capricorn, for instance, it simply means that you were born on one of the days when the Sun was in that particular astrological sign. Sun Signs are also known as Star Signs, but it means the same thing.

ASTRONOMY
VERSUS ASTROLOGY

 Derived from the Greek word *astron*, a star, astronomy and astrology study celestial phenomena, but while astronomy focuses on known scientific laws governing the physical aspects of the stars and planets, astrology concentrates on their psychological significance and their correlation with life on Earth.

Until fairly recent times, astronomy and astrology were both branches of the same subject and were taught together. Physicians, for example, were trained in both skills and consulted a patient's birth chart to aid their diagnoses of disease.

PTOLEMY (C. 90–168 C.E.) LAID THE FOUNDATIONS OF MODERN ASTROLOGY.

THE SUN AND THE MOON

 Though strictly speaking the Sun is a star and the Moon is a satellite of the planet Earth, for the purposes of astrology these two significant celestial bodies are referred to in astrological horoscopes as "planets."

THE PLANETS

The planets of our solar system are the key players in the astrological map, each one a symbol of unseen energy. Each planet rules over one, and in some cases two, signs of the zodiac, and represents qualities and characteristics that are reflected upon all those born under its influence.

CELESTIAL JOURNEYS

As the planets journey around the Sun, each traveling a unique orbit and at different speeds, they form passing links with one another that are sometimes harmonious and sometimes stressful, depending on the angular relationships they create with each other along these pathways. These links may be fleeting, as with the fast-moving Moon, or they may last several months when a slower planet, such as Pluto, is involved. The links are known as "aspects" and correspond to events taking place on the

THE INTERPLAY OF THE PLANETS REFLECTS THE PATTERN OF EVENTS ON EARTH.

Earth below – the easy aspects exert a positive influence and the stressful ones are more challenging.

*Other titles in the
Pocket Prophecy
series*

DOWSING

DREAMS

GRAPHOLOGY

I CHING

NUMEROLOGY

PALMISTRY

RUNES

TAROT

THE LUMINARIES

THE SUN: Ruler of Leo, the Sun represents our vitality, our energy, our personal, physical, and creative power. Symbolizing the ego, it highlights our talents and potential. Upon its subjects the Sun confers honor and dignity, endowing them with a sense of authority and nobility. When it is well aspected, it brings out our love and warmth, stimulates creative urge, and enhances our exuberance. When badly aspected, it encourages selfishness and conceit.

THE MOON: Because of her ever-changing shape, the Moon represents those responses and impressions that, like the Moon herself, come and go as we interact with others. Emotions come under her sway, and as she waxes and wanes, so she affects our moods and reactions. The Moon rules the sign of Cancer and is associated with water and the tides. She is the symbol of motherhood, of the creative part of life. When well aspected, she fosters our nurturing instincts, promotes sensitivity, and stimulates memory and imagination. Poorly aspected, she brings restlessness, mood swings, and a cold disposition.

THE INNER PLANETS

MERCURY: Messenger of the gods, Mercury represents communications, education, and travel, and symbolizes mental activity. Ruler of Gemini and Virgo, when well aspected, Mercury quickens the wits, promotes intelligence, shrewdness, and linguistic ability. Badly aspected, it brings out nervous energy, sarcasm, mischievousness, and mendacity.

VENUS: Venus rules Taurus and Libra. As the goddess of love, this planet rules the affections and represents beauty, pleasure, and harmony. Venus is the symbol of femininity and is associated with the arts. When well aspected, romantic prospects are increased while kindness, gentleness, and refinement come to the fore. Negative aspects bring indolence and flirtatiousness.

THE PLANET VENUS REPRESENTS ROMANTIC LOVE.

MARS: The difference between assertion and aggression depends on whether Mars is positively or negatively aspected. As the mythological god of war, Mars imparts energy, physical power, and sexual drive. It governs Aries and represents masculinity and dynamic strength. Used positively, Mars energizes and brings courage and sporting prowess. Negatively, Mars incites rudeness, and quarrelsomeness, and may lead to cruelty.

JUPITER: Ruler of Sagittarius, Jupiter is associated with opportunity and good fortune. Expansion comes under Jupiter's sway, physically, economically, and by way of extending the boundaries of our knowledge. Positively, Jupiter encourages increase, generosity, benevolence, and philosophical understanding. Negatively, it brings extravagance, self-indulgence, and over-optimism.

SATURN: Symbolizing discipline and structure, Saturn rules the sign of Capricorn and represents responsibility, stability, integrity, and old age. It demands patience, hard work, application, and a sense of duty, for which it brings just rewards. Through limitation and restriction, Saturn teaches pragmatism and maturity, and confers wisdom. Negatively, it instills stinginess, miserliness, and pessimism.

THE OUTER PLANETS

URANUS: Since its discovery by William Herschel in 1781, Uranus has been assigned rulership of Aquarius and rules over new inventions, electricity, science, technology, and space travel. Shock, revolution, and sudden change come under its sway. It sweeps away obstacles to progress and breathes new life into stagnation. Positively, it influences far-sightedness, original ideas, and humanitarian instincts. Negatively, it encourages eccentricity, rebellion, and destruction.

NEPTUNE: Named after the god of the sea, Neptune was discovered in 1846 and assigned to the rulership of Pisces. This planet's influence is subtle, nebulous, and intangible. It is the planet of illusion and escapism, and rules fantasy and dreams. Poisons and drugs come under its auspices, but so do cinematics, photography, and film. Positively, Neptune fosters mysticism, sensitivity, imagination, and poetic inspiration. Negatively, it can lead to deception and pretence.

PLUTO: Not discovered until 1930, Pluto has been assigned the rulership of Scorpio and has now come to be associated with transition and transformation. It governs the processes of elimination, symbolizing death and rebirth, endings and new beginnings, sex and regeneration. Because it brings the hidden to the surface, Pluto is linked to psychoanalysis, the paranormal, and the occult. Well aspected, it confers power of analysis, the ability to transcend the present and make a fresh start. Negatively, it can bring cruelty, sadism, and self-destruction.

PLANET	SYMBOL	RULES OVER	APPROXIMATE LENGTH OF STAY IN EACH SIGN
Sun	☉	Leo	1 month
Moon	☽	Cancer	2 ½ days
Mercury	☿	Gemini Virgo	2 – 10 weeks
Venus	♀	Taurus Libra	3 ½ weeks – 4 months
Mars	♂	Aries	2 months
Jupiter	♃	Sagittarius	1 year
Saturn	♄	Capricorn	2 ½ years
Uranus	♅	Aquarius	7 years
Neptune	♆	Pisces	14 years
Pluto	♇	Scorpio	up to 30 years

SIGNS OF THE ZODIAC

The astrological year begins at the spring equinox when the Sun enters Aries.
In historical times this was regarded as New Year's Day. The Sun remains
in each sign for one month and takes one year to travel through all twelve.

ARIES
MARCH 21 – APRIL 20

Aries is associated with leadership and new beginnings. Ruled by Mars and symbolized by the Ram, Aries is the sign of the ego.

TAURUS
APRIL 21 – MAY 20

Taurus is ruled by Venus and symbolized by the Bull. It is the sign of the builder.

GEMINI
MAY 21 – JUNE 20

Ruled by Mercury, the messenger of the gods, Gemini is symbolized by the Heavenly Twins. It is the sign of communications, language, and the intellect.

CANCER
JUNE 21 – JULY 22

The fourth sign of the Zodiac, Cancer is ruled by the Moon and symbolized by the Crab. It represents the feminine principle and is the sign of the mother, family, and the home.

LEO
JULY 23 – AUGUST 22

The fifth sign of the Zodiac, Leo is ruled by the Sun. It is symbolized by the Lion, king of all beasts, and is the sign of royalty, privilege, and rulership.

VIRGO
AUGUST 23 – SEPTEMBER 22

The sixth sign of the cycle, Virgo is ruled by Mercury and is symbolized by the young Maiden carrying a sheaf of corn. It is the sign of work and health.

LIBRA
SEPTEMBER 23 – OCTOBER 22

Ruled by Venus, Libra is the seventh sign of the Zodiac and is symbolized by the Scales of Justice. It is the sign of partnerships.

SCORPIO
OCTOBER 23 – NOVEMBER 21

Eighth in line and ruled by Pluto, the god of the Under-world, Scorpio is symbolized by the Scorpion and is the sign of power and regeneration.

SAGITTARIUS
NOVEMBER 22 – DECEMBER 21

Ruled by Jupiter, Sagittarius is the sign of the higher mind. It is symbolized by the Centaur, half-man half-beast, aiming his arrow into the distance.

CAPRICORN
DECEMBER 22 – JANUARY 19

Capricorn is ruled by Saturn, the Father of Time and task-master of the heavens. Symbolized by the Mountain Goat, it is the sign of ambition.

AQUARIUS
JANUARY 20 – FEBRUARY 18

The eleventh sign of the Zodiac and ruled by the planet Uranus, Aquarius is symbolized by Waves of either electricity or light. It is the sign of originality.

PISCES
FEBRUARY 20 – MARCH 20

Pisces is ruled by Neptune, sign of spirituality, and is sym-bolized by Two Fish joined together but swimming in opposite directions.

THE SPRING EQUINOX MARKS THE START OF THE ZODIAC YEAR.

ARIES
March 21 – April 20
THE RAM

THE TRUE ARIES

Driven by the need to be first, Aries people are fiercely competitive. They have boundless energy and are quick witted and perceptive. Arians often act on impulse, throwing themselves enthusiastically into everything they undertake. But the novelty invariably wears off, and then they're just as quick to move off to their new passion, leaving a trail of half-finished projects in their wake. Aries is a Masculine sign whose Element is Fire.

HOW TO SPOT AN ARIAN

Look for a long face with a wide forehead and thick fleecy hair. They have bodies that are strong and athletic. They wear comfortable clothes, often casual or sporty.

THE ARIES CHILD

Youngsters of this sign are live wires. Impatient to get moving, they learn to walk early – and from then on are hardly ever still! Active and energetic, they do well at sports. Keeping them busy is the key. The importance of sharing is an essential lesson they must learn.

IDEAL HOME

Keen on home improvements, Aries people are forever decorating and refurbishing their lairs. A minimalist, uncluttered look that displays souvenirs of their travels and sporting activities is preferred. Accessories in reds and pinks bring warmth into their lives.

TYPICALLY SPORTY, ARIANS HAVE STRONG ATHLETIC PHYSIQUES.

AT WORK

Challenge in a career is what they seek. Aries people are full of bright ideas and, when fired with enthusiasm, they will throw all their efforts into work. Driven, competitive, and self-motivated, they are at their best in leadership roles where they are able to mastermind new projects and delegate mundane tasks to fellow workers. Active, adventurous, physical occupations are preferred by members of this sign.

HEALTH

Aries rules the head, and many members of this sign are prone to complaints such as headaches, eye-strain, and neuralgia. Because they act impetuously, Aries people have a tendency to cause themselves injury. Due to the fiery nature of their ruling planet Mars, high fevers and acute infections are also associated with this sign.

ARIANS SEEK
ADVENTUROUS CAREERS.

MONEY

With their implusive streak, no Aries can resist a bargain, and sales draw them like magnets. They have a lucky streak, but good fortune is often of their own making. They are never afraid to stick their necks out, or to grasp a passing opportunity, so many of their risks pay off handsomely.

CAREER ROUTES

- engineering ✓
- car racing
- armed forces ✓
- sports ✓
- firefighting
- the media ✓

TAURUS
April 21 – May 20
THE BULL

THE TRUE TAURUS

Practical and down-to-earth, Taureans strive for security and stability. Routine is important in their lives, and they are terrific planners and list-makers. They like to be prepared for any eventuality, so they save money and collect possessions as anchors, tethering them against the storms of life. All Taureans delight in creature comforts and have substantial appetites for good food and fine wines. Taurus is a Feminine sign whose Element is Earth.

TAUREANS LIKE TO DRESS IN CLASSICAL STYLE.

HOW TO SPOT A TAUREAN

Look for a sturdy body, though many female Taureans have a pear-shaped figure. They are traditionalists, and it is the classical style in clothes that best suits their image, with attention sometimes drawn to the neck.

THE TAURUS CHILD

Young Taureans are easy to raise because they are placid and contented people. As long as they are warm, comfortable, and well-fed, they will gurgle away happily for hours. They enjoy making things at school and will excel in art, music, and dance. These children must be allowed to go at their own pace – pushing them too far or against their will is simply counterproductive.

IDEAL HOME

Deep comfort and luxury typifies the Taurean home. Food is where the heart is, so the kitchen will be their pride and joy. Here, classical styles predominate, and earthy tones mix happily with delicate pinks, blues, and greens.

AT WORK

Hard-working and dependable, Taureans are the backbone of the workforce. They take a practical, hands-on attitude to their work. They make excellent craftworkers, excel in the arts, are astute when involved with finances, and gifted in design. Moreover, they are able to take humdrum repetitive tasks in their stride.

HEALTH

Strong and robust, Taureans generally enjoy good health. However, a tendency to throat infections, hoarseness, or loss of voice are common problems with them. Taureans must watch their diets, since a large appetite, an enjoyment of food, and an especially sweet tooth can lead to weight gain.

MONEY

Financial security is important for Taureans, and they tend to put their money in banks or safe investments. Because they are not risk takers, they are unlikely to play the stock market. Putting their money into bricks and mortar is a safer investment and more their style.

CAREER ROUTES

- *banking*
- *agriculture*
- *fashion*
- *real estate*
- *sales*
- *the arts*

PRACTICAL WORK SUITS MEMBERS OF THIS SIGN.

> **GEMINI**
> *May 21 – June 20*
> **THE TWINS**

THE TRUE GEMINI

Versatile and adaptable, Gemini are some of the most flexible people in the Zodiac, happy to fit into whatever circumstances require. With their mercurial minds and ready wits, they can evaluate a situation in the twinkling of an eye and hold four conversations at once without losing the thread of any. A low boredom threshold demands constant stimulation and sends them in perpetual search of new interests, different people, and diverse amusements. Gemini is a Masculine sign whose Element is Air.

THE GEMINI CHILD

Insatiably curious, young Geminis want to know all about the world around them and will bombard their parents with a stream of questions. With their enquiring minds, these restless youngsters do well in languages and literature, and excel in computer work.

IDEAL HOME

Decidedly modern, the Gemini home is characterized by light and space. An apartment or loft conversion in the heart of the city would be an ideal place for them to live. Here, natural wood complements the cream and yellow decor while hi-tech gadgets, books, and magazines abound.

HOW TO SPOT A GEMINI

Look for constant motion. If they're not arriving, they're departing, and even when standing still, they can't stop fidgeting. They have bright alert eyes that don't miss a thing.

A TYPICAL GEMINI
IS RESTLESS AND ALERT.

GEMINIS ARE STRONG COMMUNICATORS.

AT WORK

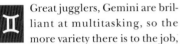 Great jugglers, Gemini are brilliant at multitasking, so the more variety there is to the job, the happier they will be. Communication is their forte, whether it be writing, demonstrating, sales, computer work, or simply giving directions. Brilliant talkers and announcers, Gemini do exceptionally well in the media.

HEALTH

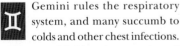 Gemini rules the respiratory system, and many succumb to colds and other chest infections. They are highly strung and tend toward a "nervy" disposition. The arms and hands are also Gemini-ruled, which leads to constant fidgeting.

CAREER ROUTES

- *journalism*
- *lecturing*
- *travel industry*
- *advertising*
- *media*
- *information technology*

MONEY

 Computer banking is tailor-made for the hi-tech whizz-kids of this sign. In fact, they probably work with computers. Gemini are not averse to taking risks and don't mind breaking the odd rule or two. They certainly have the ability to make lots of money and appreciate it for the freedom it gives them to pursue their own interests.

CANCER
June 21 – July 22
THE CRAB

THE TRUE CANCER

Just like the crab, Cancerians protect their tender emotions with a tough outer shell. Easily hurt by unkindness and injustice, they retreat into this shell at the slightest provocation, thus confirming their reputation for moodiness and bad temper. Behind the facade, though, lie kind and caring souls who are intuitive and understanding of others. Traditionalists at heart, they need security and firm roots. Cancer is a Feminine sign whose Element is Water.

CREATIVE CANCERIANS MAKE FINE WRITERS.

HOW TO SPOT A CANCERIAN

Look out for fair skin and a round face with a soft and milky-white complexion. Cancerian faces are expressive and reflect every mood and feeling as they speak. They favor conservative styles when buying clothes.

THE CANCER CHILD

Children of this sign are warm, loving youngsters who thrive on hugs. Sensitive and vulnerable, they form strong bonds with their parents, with younger siblings, with their home, pets, and possessions. A passion for collecting things develops early, so the Cancerian child's room will be crammed with personal treasures.

IDEAL HOME

Cancer people pour much love and attention into their homes and enjoy decorating and interior design. Creams and pale greens are favorite shades; silver and glass sparkle on the shelves. Cancerians are water babies, so bathrooms are usually warm and inviting.

AT WORK

Cancerians are happiest working from home, so freelance work suits them; however, they also like to feel part of a larger, protective organization. Creative and imaginative, many make fine interior designers. Writing, too, is another talent, and because many are naturally drawn to childcare, perhaps writing for children would be ideal. Hotel work and trading in antiques gives satisfaction.

HEALTH

Anatomical areas linked with this sign are the stomach, the breasts, and the upper digestive tract. Cancerians are born worriers and must learn to take a deep breath and relax, or else their fretting may cause stomach ulcers and digestive problems. Ailments associated with women are governed by this sign; however, Cancerians are no more likely to develop cancer than any other sign of the Zodiac.

MONEY

Cancerians fear putting all their money into one pot and will squirrel it away into many different saving schemes. Having a substantial cash pile gives them a sense of deep satisfaction. They like to have enough stored away to provide for a rainy day or help loved ones in need.

AUCTIONEERING WORK
ATTRACTS CANCERIANS.

CAREER ROUTES

- *auctioneering*
- *interior design*
- *writing*
- *construction work*
- *catering*
- *nursing*

LEO
☾ July 23 – August 22 ☽
THE LION

THE TRUE LEO

Born to rule, Leos are endowed with a brave heart and a proud bearing. They are colorful and dynamic people with a sunny disposition. Like their ruler, the Sun, they radiate warmth and affability, attracting by the sheer power of their magnetic personalities. Glamorous and dramatic, they are sometimes accused of arrogance when they bask in the limelight. Extravagant, they are also extremely generous. Leo is a Masculine sign whose Element is Fire.

THE LEO CHILD

Little Leos are bundles of fun. Each one is a born performer, developing precocious talents that amuse and entertain. Dressing-up is their favorite pastime. At school, they often excel in art and drama, but they shine in whatever they undertake as long as praise and encouragement are forthcoming.

LEOS JUST LOVE
BRIGHT FIERY COLORS.

IDEAL HOME

As befits the "king of the jungle," the Leo household has a palatial feel to it. Luxurious touches are a testament to expensive tastes. Gold, orange, and burnished copper are the colors that accent opulent furnishings, rich mahogany, and lush potted plants.

HOW TO SPOT A LEO

Look for high cheekbones, feline features, and a luxuriant mane of leonine hair. They hold their heads high and carry themselves with regal confidence.

RECOGNITION
AT WORK IS
IMPORTANT
TO LEOS.

AT WORK

For Leos, who are born show-men and women, all the world's a stage. In work as well as in life, they like to have fun and be the center of attention, so the entertainment business is tailor-made for them. To keep Leos happy at work, give them recognition and applause for their efforts. And remember that they like to be the boss.

HEALTH

Leo rules the heart and the spine and, therefore, heart conditions such as high blood pressure, irregular pulse, and poor circulation tend to be associated with this sign. In addition, Leos are prone to back or spinal trouble and they are advised to be careful when lifting heavy objects.

MONEY

Status and wealth are important to Leos, who need a good income to support their life-styles. They live life to the full and despise penny-pinching. They can be extravagant, but they are also acclaimed for their generosity. Leos have a gambling streak, but like all cats, they invariably land on their feet.

CAREER ROUTES

- *the theater* ✓
- *teaching* ✓
- *leisure industry* ✓
- *demonstrating*
- *business* ✓
- *designing* ✓

VIRGO
August 23 – September 22
THE MAIDEN

THE TRUE VIRGO

♍ Clever, incisive, and analytical, Virgos are sharp and observant. They are practical people, realistic in their approach to life and eager to help those in need. Yet they are critical and, with high standards and an eye for perfection, they are often too ready to find fault. Modest and cautious, members of this sign do not court the limelight, but prefer to stand on the sidelines and watch. Virgo is a Feminine sign whose Element is Earth.

HOW TO SPOT A VIRGO

Look for neatness, since Virgos are typically smart and well-groomed. They are also modest and prefer restrained, demure styles – never ostentatious or bold.

THE VIRGO CHILD

♍ With their shrewd and agile minds, Virgo youngsters don't miss a trick. They are quick learners, able to home in on details and spot things that other people miss. In addition to being mathematically gifted, they learn to read and write at an early age. Though they are generally well-behaved, they can be fussy about food.

IDEAL HOME

♍ Lovers of the understatement, Virgos choose subdued colors and tiny prints for their decor. Deep greens, chocolate browns, navy, and white contribute a classical look to their household. Proud Virgos keep their homes neat and clean.

OBSERVANT AND PRECISE, VIRGOS DELIGHT IN DETAIL.

AT WORK

♍ Sticklers for detail, Virgos make thorough and painstaking workers. Few other signs of the Zodiac can match Virgo's organizational talents and methodical approach. Service to others is their calling, so many lean toward careers in health, education, or research and development. In business, they make fine company secretaries.

HEALTH

♍ The intestines, the spleen, and the gall bladder are the sensitive anatomical areas that are associated with this sign. No wonder Virgos are notoriously fussy with food. With a tendency to intestinal complaints, they really do need to watch what they eat and make sure that their diets are as pure and natural as possible.

MONEY

♍ Virgos are money-minded and know how to make ends meet. They abhor taking financial risks and are unlikely to gamble on the stock market. They prefer to save as they earn, slowly but surely building up a nest egg for the future in the bank.

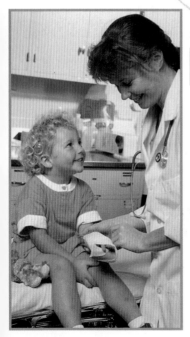

CAREER ROUTES

- *medicine*
- *research*
- *analysis*
- *teaching*
- *dietetics*
- *veterinary work*

HELPING OTHERS GIVES
VIRGOS SATISFACTION.

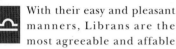

LIBRA
September 23 – October 22
THE SCALES

THE TRUE LIBRA

With their easy and pleasant manners, Librans are the most agreeable and affable people in the Zodiac. They're delightful to have around, always ready with an amusing story to tell and a sympathetic ear to listen. Tolerant and broad-minded, Librans are life's peacemakers. They dislike confrontations, rarely express anger, and are always willing to compromise. Libra is a Masculine sign whose Element is Air.

THE LIBRA CHILD

Libran children have the sort of looks that take the prize at a beautiful baby contest. They soon discover that charm, coupled with an engaging smile, can soften the hardest of hearts. At school, young Librans are popular with classmates and often distinguish themselves in music and dance.

IDEAL HOME

With their exquisite sense of style, Librans make gracious living look effortless. Balance is the key: colors are blended and patterns harmonized. Cool greens and eau-de-nil suggest timeless elegance, while music and vases of fresh flowers create an air of peace and beauty in the home.

HOW TO SPOT A LIBRAN

Look for a man who is suave and debonair, or a woman who is elegant and chic. Librans have large eyes, dimples, and heart-shaped mouths, all of which add to their attractiveness and charm.

LIBRA'S IMAGE IS POLISHED AND STYLISH.

CAREER ROUTES

- *music and dance*
- *dress design*
- *beauty industry*
- *diplomatic corp*
- *legal profession*
- *public relations*

FAIR-MINDED
LIBRANS ARE DRAWN
TO CAREERS IN LAW.

AT WORK

Whether physical or psychological, Librans shy away from messy situations, so they are drawn to white-collar occupations rather than manual labor. Their instinctive sense of fair play leads them to the judicial world, while their tact takes them into arbitration and advice. But to be truly happy, Librans must have a work environment that is both pleasant and congenial.

HEALTH

The kidneys and urinary tract are linked to this sign, and Librans may be prone to renal or bladder problems. There is also a connection between the kidneys and the ears, which means that some Librans may experience hearing problems or loss of balance at some point in their lives.

MONEY

Librans need lots of money because spending it gives them so much pleasure. And they do tend to spend their well-earned cash very freely – on stylish clothes and shoes, on personal adornments, and on beautiful objects to enhance their home space. Consequently, they sometimes find it hard to balance the books.

SCORPIO
October 23 – November 21
THE SCORPION

THE TRUE SCORPIO

Scorpio individuals are focused and intense. They tend to be secretive, and their minds, complex and deep, can be impossible to fathom. With a powerful personality and forceful determination, Scorpios allow little to stand in their way. Their temper is legendary, but their steely self-control masks a supersensitive nature. Scorpio is a Feminine sign whose Element is Water.

ENIGMATIC SCORPIOS HAVE
A SENSUOUS DRESS STYLE.

HOW TO SPOT A SCORPIO

Look for a strong build and an abundance of hair. Scorpios are dark and sultry with an air of mystery about them. But the penetrating gaze and almost hypnotic stare instantly mark them out.

THE SCORPIO CHILD

Young Scorpios may act tough, but underneath they are sensitive creatures who take teasing to heart. These children are very loyal to the people they love and form close bonds with their brothers and sisters. They have curious, inquiring minds and excel in scientific or technological subjects at school.

IDEAL HOME

Sensual, dramatic, and exotic, Scorpio's home, like its owner, tends to make a bold statement. Black is teamed with rich burgundy red; oriental touches enhance western classical styles; large mirrors reflect deep and seductive upholstery, while dimmer lights create atmosphere and mood.

AT WORK

Scorpios make top investigators, researchers, and detectives. They are brilliant sleuths and rarely give up once they are on the case. Occupations that involve the search for information, getting to the bottom of a mystery, or uncovering the truth will be a compelling draw to any Scorpio. The skillful handling of precision tools is also a special talent among them.

HEALTH

The reproductive system tends to be the weak link with Scorpios, who may be susceptible to ailments of the genitourinary system. Other illnesses from which they may suffer include sinus problems and chronic rhinitis. But as long as they can remain calm and avoid depression, Scorpios have the ability to shrug off most common disorders.

MONEY

To a Scorpio, money represents power. Scorpio individuals can be financial geniuses, making their income from a variety of different sources and often inheriting large sums of money. They rarely take risks in financial matters, and as in all things, their secretive natures mean that they like to keep their dealings to themselves.

SCORPIOS ARE DRAWN TO
CAREERS IN RESEARCH.

CAREER ROUTES

- surgery
- research
- psychoanalysis
- police work
- meat trade
- engineering

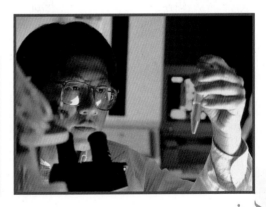

SAGITTARIUS
November 22 – December 21
THE ARCHER

THE TRUE SAGITTARIUS

Optimistic and happy-go-lucky, Sagittarians are friendly, genial people. Their buoyant cheerfulness helps them breeze through life while their philosophical approach means they can take the rough with the smooth. Restless and curious, they yearn to discover what is always out of reach. Intuitive and honest, they may be blunt, but they invariably hit the nail on the head. Sagittarius is a Masculine sign whose Element is Fire.

SAGITTARIANS
CHOOSE COMFORT
OVER STYLE.

THE SAGITTARIUS CHILD

Ever mobile, these youngsters are made for activity and adventure. They love making people laugh and from an early age will tell jokes, mimic others, and generally play the clown. At school, Sagittarian children do exceptionally well in languages, are brilliant story-tellers, and excel at sports.

IDEAL HOME

For Sagittarians, life is far too short to waste time dusting shelves, and their home will have a lived-in look. But it is always warm and welcoming, the door is usually open for visitors, and food and drink are shared generously. Books on philosophy and travel abound.

HOW TO SPOT A SAGITTARIAN

Look for a warm manner, a ready smile, and a laugh that sounds like a neighing horse. They sometimes carry excess weight on the hips and thighs. Clothes are comfortable and casual.

AT WORK

Politics, religion, and the law are the three areas traditionally associated with this sign. Eminently adaptable, Sagittarians enjoy diversity and thrive on change so a career involving travel is ideal. Above all, they are philosophers, and many will be found in colleges of higher education. Writing and publishing are favored occupations, and many follow careers in sport.

HEALTH

Generally strong and healthy, the Sagittarian weak spots are the hips and thighs, which are prone to sciatica, rheumatism, and other problems of the joints. Because they are fond of rich food and wine and have a large appetite, they may develop liverish conditions and be prone to put on weight, especially in later life.

SAGITTARIANS LOVE TO ROAM
SO A CAREER INVOLVING
TRAVEL WOULD SUIT
THEIR NATURE WELL.

CAREER ROUTES

- *travel industry*
- *publishing*
- *foreign languages*
- *higher education*
- *the law*
- *sport*

MONEY

Archers of all ages take a fairly philosophical attitude to money. Easy-come, easy-go is their motto, but then they can afford to think like this since theirs is the luckiest sign in the Zodiac. Naturally daring and far-sighted, they rarely balk at taking financial risks – after all, Lady Luck is usually on their side.

CAPRICORN
December 22 – January 19
THE GOAT

HOW TO SPOT A CAPRICORN

Look for a bony, angular frame. The face is often long, and the forehead may be deeply furrowed. When they are young, they look much older than their years, but conversely, they appear to grow younger as they age.

THE TRUE CAPRICORN

Capricorns tend to be conservative and uphold traditional values: sensible, serious, and sober-minded. Reputation and good standing are important to them, for they are ambitious, status-conscious, and achievement-motivated. They strive for success because failure is unthinkable. Scholarly and disciplined, Capricorn people are some of the best organizers in the Zodiac. Capricorn is a Feminine sign whose Element is Earth.

THE CAPRICORN CHILD

Born with an old head on young shoulders, youngsters of this sign resent being treated as children. In fact, they prefer the company of older people to that of their own age group. At school, they work hard and become prefects or monitors. Capricorn children are often too serious and need to be tickled once in a while.

IDEAL HOME

Classical and formal describes the Capricorn's home. They are dedicated to housework so there will not be a single speck of dust anywhere. Here, quality rather

SERIOUS AND SOBER,
CAPRICORNS ARE
TRADITIONALISTS
AT HEART.

than quantity is the norm, with valuable antiques taking prominence. A gray color scheme adds the final touches of sophistication.

AT WORK

Responsible and industrious, Capricorn individuals work hard for their living. They take their work extremely seriously, and many are workaholics. They are fiercely ambitious and set their minds on reaching the top of their chosen career. Most enjoy the cut-and-thrust of business and are likely to be found in executive positions or on the company board.

BUSINESS AND MANAGEMENT
ATTRACTS CAPRICORNS.

HEALTH

The skin, teeth, knees, and all bones are the vulnerable areas associated with this sign. Capricorn people are prone to rashes, gout, stiffness of the joints, and fractures. Hearing, too, may be a problem. Though Capricorns may lack stamina when they are young, this sign is known for its longevity.

MONEY

For goal-oriented Capricorn, making money is perhaps the fundamental drive in life. These hard-working, conscientious people never miss an opportunity to increase their savings and will work every hour of the day to increase their wealth.

CAREER ROUTES

- *administration*
- *management*
- *big business*
- *economics*
- *banking*
- *public sector*

AQUARIUS
January 20 — February 18
THE WATER CARRIER

THE TRUE AQUARIUS

Original and avant-garde, Aquarians are unconventional people. Fundamentally individualistic, creative, and inspired, they take a fresh approach to contemporary issues and invariably come up with revolutionary answers. Tolerant and broad-minded, they are driven by humanitarian ideals, and the Aquarian motto must surely be: live and let live. Natives of this sign are sociable and popular, and have a wide network of friends. Aquarius is a Masculine sign whose Element is Air.

THE AQUARIUS CHILD

Children of this sign are intelligent with inventive minds. They want to know what makes the world tick and are fascinated by anything experimental. At school, they do well in science and technology, and often ask questions that baffle the teachers. Not the cuddliest of children, they do, nevertheless, need lots of friends.

IDEAL HOME

The Aquarian home is as unconventional as its owner, for this is the house of the post-modernist, and it will be filled with the unusual and the eccentric. Glass and chrome, hi-tech instruments, and space-age gadgets will prevail. Turquoise or electric-blue form part of the color scheme.

HOW TO SPOT AN AQUARIAN

Look for an attractive face with a distinctive profile. But it is the Aquarian's unusual dress sense that often marks them out from the crowd.

AQUARIAN STYLE
IS HIGHLY INDIVIDUAL.

AQUARIANS FAVOR
CAREERS THAT
ARE OUT OF THE
ORDINARY.

AT WORK

The more unusual the job, the better Aquarians will like it. Though independent-minded, members of this sign actively choose to work with groups. Charitable organizations or community projects are a particular attraction. Aquarius is linked with electricity, with technology and with broadcasting. Working with computers or in television could be ideal for them.

HEALTH

A tendency to worry easily upsets the nervous system of Aquarians and may lead to high blood pressure. Other areas traditionally linked with Aquarius are the legs, shins, and ankles. Varicose veins,

CAREER ROUTES

- *space technology* • *tv and radio*
- *new inventions* • *charity work*
- *research and development*

sprains, and injuries to calves may be common complaints.

MONEY

Sometimes rich and sometimes poor, Aquarians make and spend money in fits and starts. Their humanitarian instincts encourage them to spread their money around for the benefit of all. Many live on a tight budget for years and then, as if by magic, are dealt an amazing stroke of luck that reverses their fortunes overnight.

PISCES

February 19 – March 20

THE FISH

THE TRUE PISCES

Dominated by emotion and intuition, Pisceans have a distinct air of other-worldliness. Their gift for picking up the feelings of others allows them to respond instinctively to problems. Never wanting to court the limelight, they are happy to go with the flow. Charming and funny, Pisceans can appear frail, yet they possess tremendous inner strength. Pisces is a Feminine sign whose Element is Water.

PISCEANS HAVE A
DELICATE, DREAMY LOOK.

HOW TO SPOT A PISCEAN

Look for eyes that are soft and limpid, often grey-green in color and turning down sleepily at the corners. They often possess a faraway, dreamy look.

THE PISCES CHILD

Soft, sensitive, and tender, Piscean children are dreamy little things with their heads in the clouds of a magical world of make-believe. At school, they daydream when lessons are boring or become difficult. But with such fertile imaginations, they write wonderful stories and paint fabulous pictures.

IDEAL HOME

A house overlooking the ocean is every Piscean's dream. In town or country, this home will somehow have connections with water – aquamarine color schemes, fish motifs, or seashells on the shelf. Comfortable and relaxed, the Piscean's home contains an eclectic mix of styles that creates a pleasingly informal setting.

AT WORK

Pisceans are multitalented people. Inherent compassion leads many into the caring professions, while innate intuition is used with stunning success in both orthodox and complementary medicine and therapy. Creative Pisceans are drawn to the world of film, to music, literature, and the arts. Those with a scientific nature do well in the chemical industries.

HEALTH

The feet are the vulnerable area for Pisces. Psychologically, however, Pisceans easily succumb to depression and other mental problems when under severe pressure or if they feel unsupported and unloved. Harmony and tranquility are essential to their health and wellbeing.

MONEY

More spiritual than materialistic, Pisces are not the best money managers in the world. Unfailingly generous, they like to share money when they have it with loved ones or give it to those less well off than themselves. They do, however, have the ability to make lots of money through their sought-after artistic talents, but need an honest adviser to help invest it wisely.

WRITING FICTION SUITS THE
PISCEAN TEMPERAMENT.

CAREER ROUTES

- *movie industry* ✓
- *psychotherapy*
- *petrochemicals*
- *romantic fiction* ✓
- *brewery trade*
- *art and design* ✓

HOW THE SIGNS INTER-RELATE

In addition to determining your personality traits, your star sign and ruling planet will influence how you build friendly or romantic relationships with others. The next section outlines your compatibility with other star signs, so read on to find out if you are really suited to your mate.

ARIES IN LOVE

Warm, affectionate, and demonstrative, Aries are passionate people who fall madly in love at first sight – and then realize the implications. The excitement of the chase thrills them and keeps love burning brightly. What will dim their ardor, though, is boredom, so they need partners who will present them with a constant challenge. In such a partnership, Aries can be loyal as well as generous and supportive; but in all their relationships, they like to take the lead and establish rules that must be obeyed. Honest and direct, Aries can sometimes be tactless and insensitive. Learning to compromise would foster greater harmony with others.

HOW COMPATIBLE IS ARIES?
match your sign

ARIES WITH:
Aries	☆☆☆☆☆
Taurus	☆☆☆
Gemini	☆☆☆☆
Cancer	☆
Leo	☆☆☆☆☆
Virgo	☆☆
Libra	☆☆☆
Scorpio	☆☆☆☆
Sagittarius	☆☆☆☆☆
Capricorn	☆☆☆☆
Aquarius	☆☆
Pisces	☆

STAR RATING:
☆ = *little in common*
☆☆ = *challenging*
☆☆☆ = *lots of attraction*
☆☆☆☆ = *well suited*
☆☆☆☆☆ = *special rapport*

TAUREAN LOVE
IS STABLE AND
ENDURING.

TAURUS IN LOVE

Taureans take time committing themselves to someone they like, but they do not play emotional games. They seek an uncomplicated relationship with a solid, trustworthy partner who will work beside them to achieve a stable, materially secure existence. Only when sure that they have found the right mate will they give loyalty and love. Sensual and pleasure-loving, Taureans adore being pampered. Although not always verbally demonstrative, they are deeply caring and highly charged sexually. Taureans are steadfast and true, but they can also be jealous and overprotective of their partners, and sometimes of friends and family, too.

HOW COMPATIBLE IS TAURUS?
match your sign

TAURUS WITH:
Aries	☆☆☆
Taurus	☆☆☆
Gemini	☆
Cancer	☆☆☆
Leo	☆☆☆
Virgo	☆☆☆☆☆
Libra	☆☆☆
Scorpio	☆☆☆
Sagittarius	☆☆
Capricorn	☆☆☆☆☆
Aquarius	☆
Pisces	☆☆☆

STAR RATING:
☆ = *little in common*
☆☆ = *challenging*
☆☆☆ = *lots of attraction*
☆☆☆☆ = *well suited*
☆☆☆☆☆ = *special rapport*

GEMINI IN LOVE

Ⅱ Amusing and intelligent, sociable and gregarious, Gemini make friends easily, and get along with almost everyone. However, they find it difficult to commit themselves to one person for a whole lifetime. Fidelity is not their strongest suit, and they can be flirtatious, falling in and out of love very quickly. Monotony and repetition depress them, so the person who wins their heart needs to be interesting and independent, someone who keeps them guessing and who is, above all, tolerant and broad-minded. With such a partner, Gemini are capable of immense love, sparkling companionship, and a guarantee that there will never be a dull moment.

HOW COMPATIBLE IS GEMINI?
match your sign

GEMINI WITH:
Aries ☆☆☆
Taurus ☆
Gemini ☆☆☆☆☆
Cancer ☆
Leo ☆☆
Virgo ☆☆☆
Libra ☆☆☆☆☆
Scorpio ☆
Sagittarius ☆☆☆
Capricorn ☆
Aquarius ☆☆☆☆
Pisces ☆☆

STAR RATING:
☆ = *little in common*
☆☆ = *challenging*
☆☆☆ = *lots of attraction*
☆☆☆☆ = *well suited*
☆☆☆☆☆ = *special rapport*

CHARMING YET FICKLE, GEMINIS LOVE TO FLIRT.

CANCERIANS BRING
ROMANCE TO THEIR
RELATIONSHIP.

HOW COMPATIBLE IS CANCER?
match your sign

CANCER WITH:

Aries	☆
Taurus	☆☆☆☆
Gemini	☆
Cancer	☆☆☆☆
Leo	☆☆☆
Virgo	☆☆☆☆
Libra	☆☆
Scorpio	☆☆☆☆☆
Sagittarius	☆☆
Capricorn	☆☆☆
Aquarius	☆
Pisces	☆☆☆☆☆

STAR RATING:
☆ = *little in common*
☆☆ = *challenging*
☆☆☆ = *lots of attraction*
☆☆☆☆ = *well suited*
☆☆☆☆☆ = *special rapport*

CANCER IN LOVE

Loyal, affectionate, and supportive, Cancerians are romantic people who are eager to love and be loved in return. Above all, they need to feel needed, for Cancerians are born to nurture others; and their soft, compassionate hearts go out to all who are lonely and distressed. They seek a true soulmate, a special person who will reassure them and who is able to calm their own doubts and fears; above all, they seek help to shield them from the uncertainties of change. Cancerians believe in domestic values, traditional roles, and old-fashioned honor; in love, they give their hearts completely and cling tightly to their mates. Though caring and protective of those they love, they can be touchy and quick to take offense, and family and friends should recognize their sensitivity and learn to avoid hurting their feelings.

LEO IN LOVE

Warm, demonstrative, and generous with their affections, Leos enjoy passion on a grand scale. They are born for love and thrive on emotional highs. A lonely, disillusioned Lion is a sorry sight indeed. Leo individuals need a partner they can be proud of, someone who, through looks or talents, will boost their ego. But they also need to be the dominant partner in any relationship, and they will not take second place. Pride can be a downfall with Leos, and they suffer if they feel they are not receiving the admiration they deserve. They find criticism deeply wounding and despise all pettiness. But Leos have hearts of gold and give themselves completely to the ones they love – their loyalty and devotion know no bounds.

LOVE IS PASSIONATE AND GRAND IN THE HANDS OF LEO.

HOW COMPATIBLE IS LEO?
match your sign

LEO WITH:

Aries	☆☆☆☆☆
Taurus	☆☆☆
Gemini	☆☆
Cancer	☆☆☆
Leo	☆☆☆☆☆
Virgo	☆
Libra	☆
Scorpio	☆☆☆☆
Sagittarius	☆☆☆☆☆
Capricorn	☆☆☆
Aquarius	☆☆☆
Pisces	☆☆☆

STAR RATING:
☆ = little in common
☆☆ = challenging
☆☆☆ = lots of attraction
☆☆☆☆ = well suited
☆☆☆☆☆ = special rapport

VIRGO SEEKS A
LIKE-MINDED SOUL-MATE.

**HOW COMPATIBLE
IS VIRGO?**
match your sign

VIRGO WITH:
Aries ✰✰
Taurus ✰✰✰✰✰
Gemini ✰✰✰
Cancer ✰✰✰✰
Leo ✰
Virgo ✰✰✰✰✰
Libra ✰
Scorpio ✰✰
Sagittarius ✰
Capricorn ✰✰✰✰✰
Aquarius ✰✰
Pisces ✰✰✰

STAR RATING:
✰ = *little in common*
✰✰ = *challenging*
✰✰✰ = *lots of attraction*
✰✰✰✰ = *well suited*
✰✰✰✰✰ = *special rapport*

VIRGO IN LOVE

When looking for love, the discriminating nature of the Virgo individual always puts brains before beauty. They are more likely to be turned on by a clever mind than a pretty face or hunky torso. Virgos may seem cool and undemonstrative, but they are very choosy in their selection of friends and lovers, and do not fall head over heels at first sight.

Theirs is a practical approach to matters of the heart, and the Virgo individual will spend time assessing carefully the pros and cons of a relationship before offering their affections. They seek someone that they can respect, a person who is intelligent, organized, and totally on the same wavelength as themselves. Such a person will find a Virgo partner not only faithful, reliable, and true in a relationship, but infinitely wise and witty, too.

ROMANCE IS THE BEST
WAY TO A LIBRAN'S HEART.

LIBRA IN LOVE

Librans are team players who dislike being alone and function best in a relationship. Rarely short of friends, it is a special, one-to-one partnership that brings them true contentment. And yet they can be cool and distant, and run a mile from emotional entanglements. They detest arguments and would rather find a compromise than embroil themselves in conflict. Born romantics, Librans spend their lives in love with love itself. For them, pleasant companionship far outweighs the earthier, more robust side of physical relationships. Appearances matter hugely, so a partner must be attractive, well-mannered, and look good at all times. Charming and easygoing, Librans attract suitors like bees to honey.

**HOW COMPATIBLE
IS LIBRA?**
match your sign

LIBRA WITH:

Aries	☆☆☆
Taurus	☆☆☆
Gemini	☆☆☆☆☆
Cancer	☆
Leo	☆
Virgo	☆
Libra	☆☆☆
Scorpio	☆☆☆
Sagittarius	☆☆
Capricorn	☆
Aquarius	☆☆☆☆☆
Pisces	☆☆☆☆

STAR RATING:
☆ = *little in common*
☆☆ = *challenging*
☆☆☆ = *lots of attraction*
☆☆☆☆ = *well suited*
☆☆☆☆☆ = *special rapport*

SCORPIO IN LOVE

With their magnetic sexuality and brooding air of mystery, Scorpio individuals are deeply attractive and never short of admirers. But love is a serious matter for these are intense and passionate people. They may have seductive personalities, but they are not given to emotional games or casual flings. Nor is it easy for them to discuss their feelings, so they may come across as cool and disinterested. Yet Scorpios are capable of such depth of feeling that few can ever hope to understand them. Scorpios give themselves completely, body and soul, to those whom they love, but they demand total commitment from their partners in return. For them, honesty and trust are paramount in a relationship, while betrayal is treason. Jealousy can be a problem, and hell hath no fury like a Scorpio crossed in love.

WHEN SCORPIOS LOVE, THEY GIVE BODY AND SOUL.

HOW COMPATIBLE IS SCORPIO?
match your sign

SCORPIO WITH:

Aries	✩✩✩✩	✓
Taurus	✩✩✩	
Gemini	✩	
Cancer	✩✩✩✩✩	✓
Leo	✩✩✩✩	✓
Virgo	✩✩	
Libra	✩✩✩	
Scorpio	✩✩✩✩	✓
Sagittarius	✩	
Capricorn	✩✩✩✩	✓
Aquarius	✩	
Pisces	✩✩✩✩✩	✓

STAR RATING:
✩ = *little in common*
✩✩ = *challenging*
✩✩✩ = *lots of attraction*
✩✩✩✩ = *well suited*
✩✩✩✩✩ = *special rapport*

SAGITTARIANS ARE
DEEPLY RESPECTFUL
TO THOSE THEY LOVE.

HOW COMPATIBLE IS SAGITTARIUS?
match your sign

SAGITTARIUS WITH:

Aries	☆☆☆☆
Taurus	☆☆
Gemini	☆☆☆
Cancer	☆☆
Leo	☆☆☆☆☆
Virgo	☆
Libra	☆☆
Scorpio	☆
Sagittarius	☆☆☆☆☆
Capricorn	☆
Aquarius	☆☆☆
Pisces	☆

STAR RATING:
☆ = *little in common*
☆☆ = *challenging*
☆☆☆ = *lots of attraction*
☆☆☆☆ = *well suited*
☆☆☆☆☆ = *special rapport*

SAGITTARIUS IN LOVE

Restless and freedom-loving, Sagittarian individuals find long-term relationships pretty daunting. They cannot bear to be tied down. Sagittarians are reluctant to commit themselves too soon in their lives, and instead they prefer to retain their independence and play the field before settling down. With their easygoing manner and their casual approach to life, they make wonderful friends – kind-hearted, good-humored, and genial. Sagittarians have a code of honor, and are chivalrous and noble toward the opposite sex.

In a partner they look for an adventurous and spunky soulmate, someone who is good-natured and shares their love of spontaneity. Passionate, honest, and outspoken, a Sagittarian mate will be totally sincere, even if somewhat tactless now and then.

CAPRICORN IN LOVE

A sense of duty and a fierce drive to achieve a position of authority often means that Capricorns put work before romance. Long hours at the office leave them little time to socialize, and thus they limit their chances of meeting potential partners. It is fortunate, then, that so many Capricorns find their soulmates at work. In love, they can be shy and awkward. They may appear unemotional on the surface, but deep inside lies a richly sentimental core. Capricorns take their commitments seriously: they are towers of strength and make excellent providers. An ideal partner for Capricorn is someone who they can respect, who is loyal, industrious, and able to help ease away the stresses of their day. To such a mate, a Capricorn will remain ever loyal and true.

HOW COMPATIBLE IS CAPRICORN?
match your sign

CAPRICORN WITH:
Aries	☆☆☆
Taurus	☆☆☆☆
Gemini	☆
Cancer	☆☆☆
Leo	☆☆☆
Virgo	☆☆☆☆☆
Libra	☆
Scorpio	☆☆☆☆
Sagittarius	☆
Capricorn	☆☆☆☆☆
Aquarius	☆
Pisces	☆☆

STAR RATING:
☆ = *little in common*
☆☆ = *challenging*
☆☆☆ = *lots of attraction*
☆☆☆☆ = *well suited*
☆☆☆☆☆ = *special rapport*

WORKAHOLIC CAPRICORNS NEED SOMEONE TO RELAX WITH.

HOW COMPATIBLE IS AQUARIUS?
match your sign

AQUARIUS WITH:
Aries	☆☆☆
Taurus	☆
Gemini	☆☆☆☆☆
Cancer	☆
Leo	☆☆☆
Virgo	☆☆
Libra	☆☆☆☆☆
Scorpio	☆
Sagittarius	☆☆☆
Capricorn	☆
Aquarius	☆☆☆☆
Pisces	☆☆

STAR RATING:
☆ = *little in common*
☆☆ = *challenging*
☆☆☆ = *lots of attraction*
☆☆☆☆ = *well suited*
☆☆☆☆☆ = *special rapport*

AQUARIANS THRIVE ON OPENNESS IN ANY RELATIONSHIP.

AQUARIUS IN LOVE

To many Aquarians, a meeting of minds can be far more stimulating than physical involvement, though this is not to say that they avoid sexual relationships. Rather, they view love with detachment: an interesting experience to be analyzed intellectually rather than plunged into emotionally. Friendship and being on the same wavelength are the most important aspects of an Aquarian's intimacy with another person. Progressive and broad-minded where sex is concerned, many Aquarians form open, or unconventional, partnerships. Jealousy is not a word that they recognize, for they are neither possessive of their partners nor do they appreciate being possessed by another. A person who is offbeat, independent, and does not cling to them makes an ideal companion for an Aquarian.

PISCES IN LOVE

Born for romance, love to a Pisces is food and drink. Dreamy and gentle Pisceans escape into a fantasy land of fairytale princesses and heroic knights, and then spend their lives trying to match the illusion to reality. Caring and sharing with a special soulmate is what Pisces yearns to do. Loneliness for them is such a wretched existence that some latch onto unsuitable partners rather than be alone. Male or female, Pisces tends to be emotional and clingy, and needs a strong partner for support. Someone who is capable yet tender, spiritual yet worldly, decisive yet sensitive enough to share their dreams, makes an ideal match for them. To such a partner, Pisces gives a lifetime of devotion and love.

HOW COMPATIBLE IS PISCES?
match your sign

PISCES WITH:
Aries	☆
Taurus	☆☆☆
Gemini	☆☆
Cancer	☆☆☆☆☆
Leo	☆☆☆
Virgo	☆☆☆
Libra	☆☆☆☆
Scorpio	☆☆☆☆☆
Sagittarius	☆
Capricorn	☆☆
Aquarius	☆☆
Pisces	☆☆☆☆☆

STAR RATING:
☆ = *little in common*
☆☆ = *challenging*
☆☆☆ = *lots of attraction*
☆☆☆☆ = *well suited*
☆☆☆☆☆ = *special rapport*

PISCEANS ENJOY DOING EVERYTHING WITH A PARTNER.

PLANNING A BIRTH CHART

A horoscope in a magazine or newspaper focuses mainly on the Sun's activity, and its forecast needs to be fairly general to be appropriate for thousands of readers at once. But a birth chart is unique to the querent and offers real guidance to the future.

IN ANCIENT TIMES

A personal horoscope requires a great deal of intricate mathematical computation. In ancient times an astrologer was present at the birth of a child and, at the first cry, scanned the heavens and noted the planet rising in the east. He then laboriously plotted the position of the Sun, the Moon, and of other celestial bodies in order to cast a birth chart.

Nowadays we have remarkable computer programs that are able to perform this task at the click of a button, and that guarantee exceptional precision as well.

THE BIRTH CHART

To construct a birth chart, three basic pieces of information are required: the date, place, and exact time of birth. If the time of birth is not known, then a chart for midday is drawn up. Although this is not ideal, it still offers a closer analysis than you would receive from a general Sun Sign reading alone.

The three pieces of information – the date, geographical longitude and latitude, and moment of birth – are converted into what is known as Sidereal, or Star, Time. The position of the planets for any date, as well as the phases of the Moon and other important cosmic phenomena, are contained in charts called

ASTROLOGICAL SYMBOLS	
The Planets	*The Signs*
☉ Sun	♈ Aries
☽ Moon	♉ Taurus
☿ Mercury	♊ Gemini
♀ Venus	♋ Cancer
♂ Mars	♌ Leo
♃ Jupiter	♍ Virgo
♄ Saturn	♎ Libra
♅ Uranus	♏ Scorpio
♆ Neptune	♐ Sagittarius
♇ Pluto	♑ Capricorn
	♒ Aquarius
	♓ Pisces

	WHAT THE HOUSES REPRESENT
1	the ego, the temperament, how the individual comes across to others
2	money, income, possessions
3	communications, short journeys, mental ability, siblings, neighbors
4	the home, parents, property
5	children, creative talents, love affairs, sport, gambling, fun and games
6	daily routines, work, health
7	marriage, partnerships, contracts
8	legacies, inheritances, sex
9	longer journeys, overseas travel, higher education, religion, legal matters
10	career, worldly aspirations, profession, one's boss, fame
11	friends, social activities, links with clubs and societies
12	dreams, innermost feelings, secrets, enemies, self-undoing

Ephemerides, and these enable the astrologer to plot the planets in their exact zodiacal positions that show the signs and sectors of the Zodiac in which they were located at the precise moment of birth.

These positions are then written into a chart resembling a wheel divided into twelve sectors, known as houses. This chart, when complete, is the symbolic representation of the individual, the querent (or situation, or event in question), and the analysis of it is based on these planetary positions, on their relationships (or aspects) to one another, their location in the different sectors, and the patterns that are formed inside the wheel.

INTERPRETING A BIRTH CHART

Elvis Presley's birth chart is based on his date of birth, January 8, 1935,
time, 4:35 A.M., and place, Tupelo, Mississippi. The position of the signs,
houses, and planets has been calculated and drawn into the wheel using
astrological symbols for convenience.

READING THE CHART

 Read from the left-hand side
of the chart where the first
house is placed. The rest of the
houses follow in a counterclockwise
direction. The dividing lines between
the houses are known as cusps, and
the astrological signs that are assigned
to each cusp depend for their position on the individual's time of birth.
Two people born on the same day
would have very different signs on
their respective first house cusps if
one, say, was born at dawn and the
other in the evening.

Each house represents a different
aspect of the individual's life, with
the sign on its cusp and any planets
in its sector highlighting and

affecting the affairs of that house.
Not all the houses will be tenanted,
but those containing several planets
are especially emphasized and show
areas that are dominant or more
important in the person's life.

Numbers showing the exact
degree positions are written beside
the planet symbols and sign symbols.
These degree positions are important, not only because they allow the
astrologer to plot them in the wheel,
but because they let us to see at a
glance the kind of relationship
patterns, the stresses and strains, the
harmonious links, the encouragement, challenges, and so on, that are
being exerted by the chart positions
– and that will therefore be mirrored
in that person's life.

ELVIS PRESLEY'S CHART

In Elvis Presley's chart, Mars the dynamic planet of energy and symbol of raw, hot-blooded masculinity, is in his 10th house of fame confirming his charismatic appeal. Jupiter, his own personal planet as ruler of his rising sign, is placed in the 11th house and pinpoints his high media profile, singing in clubs and other social venues. But it is his second house of money that is heavily tenanted by a stellium, that is, three or more planets in a cluster. Since the Sun, Mercury, and Venus, all benign and lucky influences, are involved, it is no surprise that Elvis Presley's profession in the music business brought him great fame and vast wealth.

ELVIS PRESLEY WAS BORN TO SUCCEED.

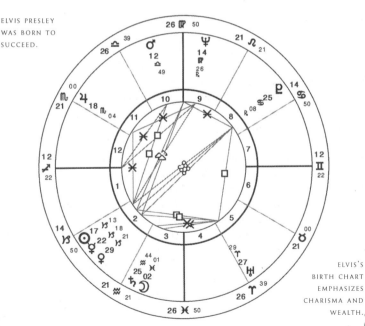

ELVIS'S BIRTH CHART EMPHASIZES CHARISMA AND WEALTH.

WHAT ASTROLOGY CAN DO FOR YOU

ARMED AND READY

Experienced astrologers can unravel the physical and psychological factors that shape and affect your life; profile your emotional needs and expectations; give insight into your hopes, dreams, and motivations; and bring to light your potential and buried talents. The astrologer can also indicate the trends likely to occur in the future by studying the movements and progression of the planets, so that you can prepare for the unexpected.

OTHER BRANCHES

There are other branches of astrology that are less well-known but equally valuable. Synastry, for example, compares the birth charts of two people to assess their compatibility. It is useful for social and intimate relationships, as well as business partnerships. Electional astrology seeks the most

THE ANSWERS YOU SEEK
ARE TO BE FOUND IN THE SKIES.

propitious moment to start a new venture, take a trip, or set up a new company. Horary astrology answers specific questions where time is a factor; mundane astrology deals with world events; financial astrology traces patterns that influence the money markets and business world; and medical astrology concerns itself with health and disease.

FURTHER READING

TOMPKINS, Sue, *Aspects in Astrology* (Element, 1989)

BIRKBECK, Lyn, *Do It Yourself Astrology* (Element, 1999)

HUNTLEY, Janis, *The Elements of Astrology* (Element, 1990)

MANN, A. T., *Life Time Astrology* (Element, 1984)

LEMESURIER, Peter, *Gospel Of The Stars* (Element, 1990)

KING, Teri, *Teri King's Complete Guide To Your Stars* (Element, 1995)

HUNTLEY, Janis, *The Complete Illustrated Guide To Astrology* (Element, 1999)

PARKER, Julia and Derek, *Parker's Astrology* (Dorling Kindersley, 1991)

CAMPION, Nicholas, *The Practical Astrologer* (Hamlyn, 1987)

OTHER ELEMENT BOOKS BY LORI REID
East West Astrology (1999)
The Elements of Hand Reading (1994)
Sweet Dreamer (1998)
The Dream Catcher (1997)

USEFUL ADDRESSES

THE FACULTY OF ASTROLOGICAL STUDIES
54 High Street
Orpington
Kent BR6 OJG, U.K.

THE ASTROLOGICAL ASSOCIATION
396 Caledonian Road
London N1 1DN
U.K.

AMERICAN FEDERATION OF ASTROLOGERS
Robert Cowper, Executive Secretary
PO Box 22040
Tempe
AZ 85285 2040
U.S.A.

ASSOCIATION FOR ASTROLOGICAL NETWORKING
8306 Wilshire Blvd
Suite 537
Beverley Hills
CA 90211
U.S.A.

INDEX